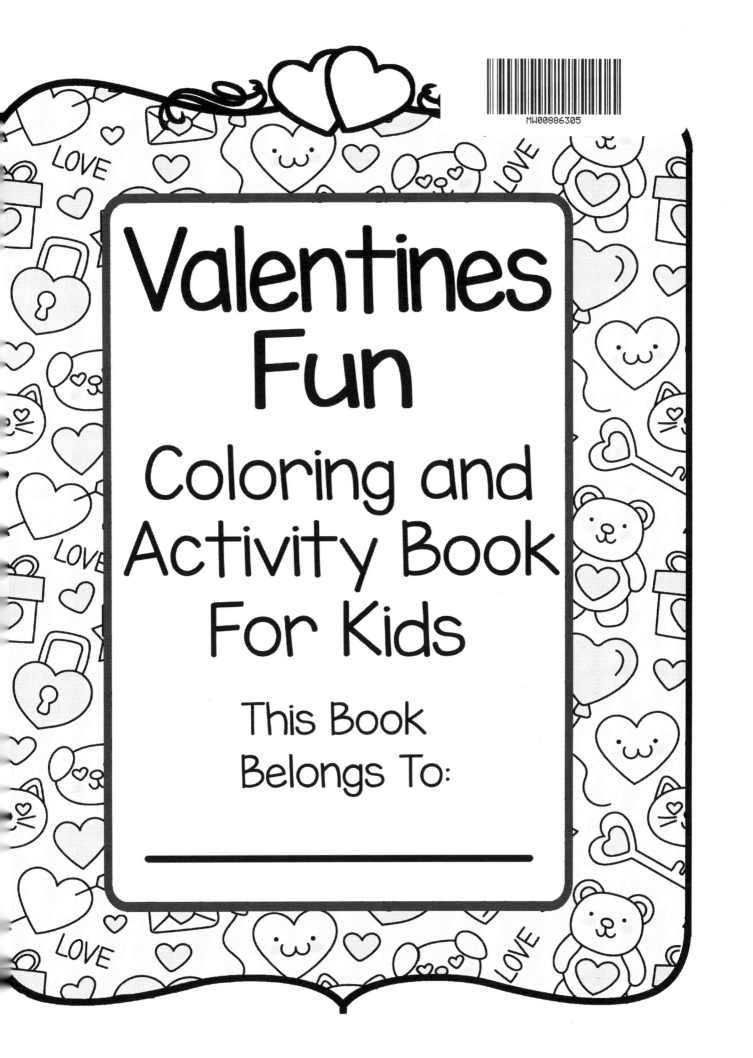

Valentines Fun

Coloring and Activity Book For Kids

This Book Belongs To:

_____

MW00886305

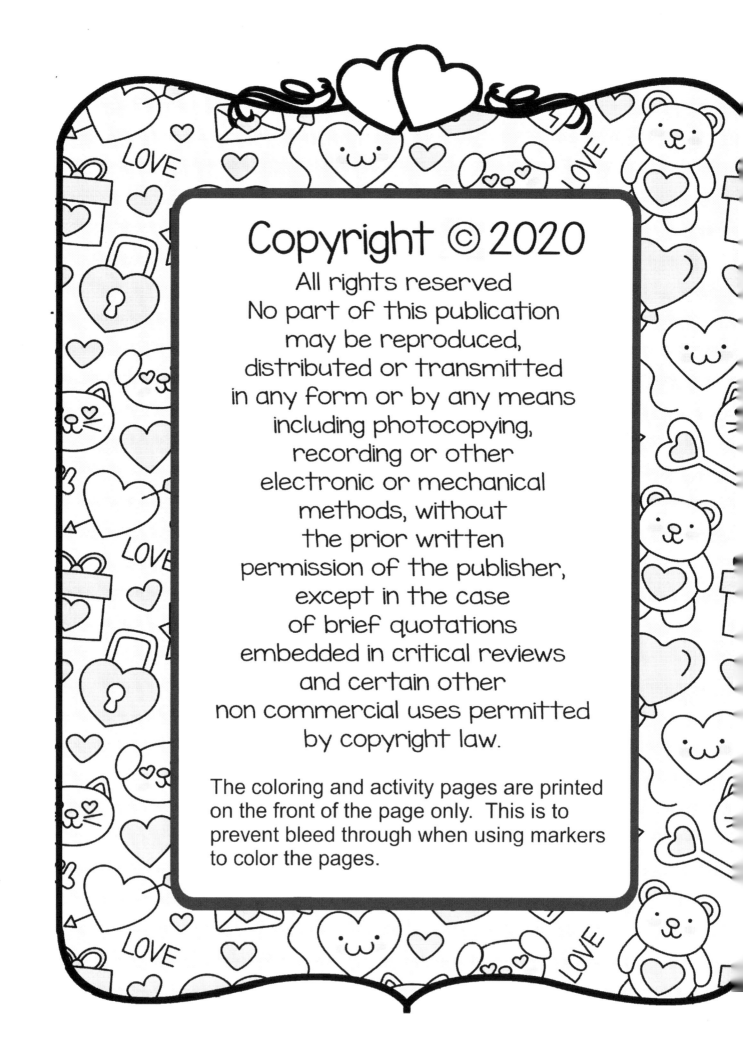

Copyright © 2020

All rights reserved
No part of this publication
may be reproduced,
distributed or transmitted
in any form or by any means
including photocopying,
recording or other
electronic or mechanical
methods, without
the prior written
permission of the publisher,
except in the case
of brief quotations
embedded in critical reviews
and certain other
non commercial uses permitted
by copyright law.

The coloring and activity pages are printed on the front of the page only. This is to prevent bleed through when using markers to color the pages.

Count How Many

Count how many there are;
Draw a (circle) around the number of how many you counted
Color the pictures.

1 one   2 two   3 three   4 four   5 five

6 six   7 seven   8 eight   9 nine   10 ten

Practice writing the number on the lines below.

_____

. . . .

_____

Trace and Color Shapes

Carefully trace each shape with a crayon. or marker.
Choose another crayon and color the inside of the shape.

Diamond

Through the Maze

Help find the way through the maze.

START

LOVE

FINISH

Match The Same

Draw a line to match the pictures that are the <u>same.</u>
Color the pictures.

Drawing Curvy Lines

Trace over the line with your pencil, then keep going.
Fill the page with curvy lines.

Color the shpes that you have made.

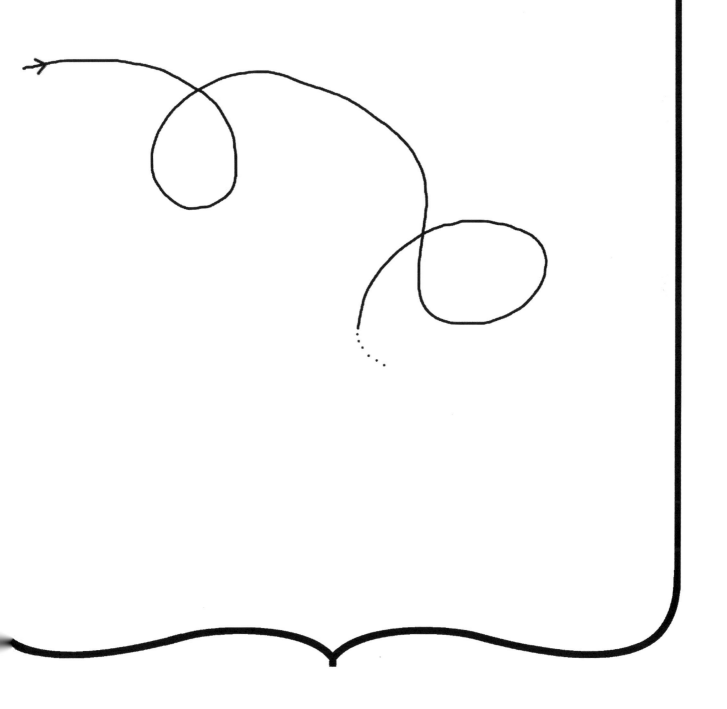

Tic - Tac - Toe

Two players decide if they want to be X or 0.
Players take turns marking the spaces in the grid with their X or 0.
The winner is the one who places three of their X's or 0's in a horizontal, vertical, or diagonal row.

Play a Tic-Tac-Toe game in each heart grid.

Count How Many

Count how many there are;
Draw a (circle) around the number of how many you counted
Color the pictures.

1 one   2 two   3 three   4 four   5 five

6 six   7 seven   8 eight   9 nine   10 ten

Practice writing the number on the lines below.

Trace and Color Shapes

Carefully trace each shape with a crayon. or marker.
Choose another crayon and color the inside of the shape.

Triangle

Through the Maze

Help find the way through the maze.

START

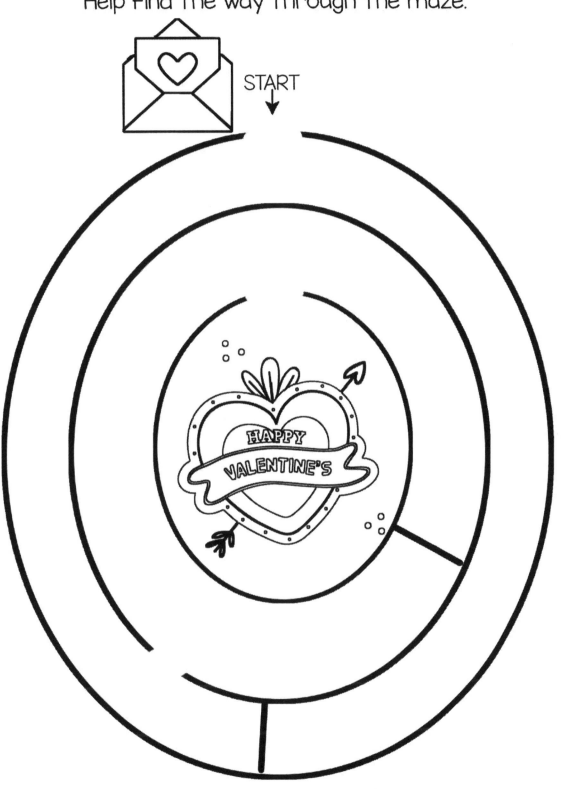

Odd One Out

Look at the first picture on each line.
Draw an X on the picture that is different.
Color the pictures.

Drawing Straight Lines

Trace over the line with your pencil, then keep going.
Fill the page with straight lines.

Color the shpes that you have made.

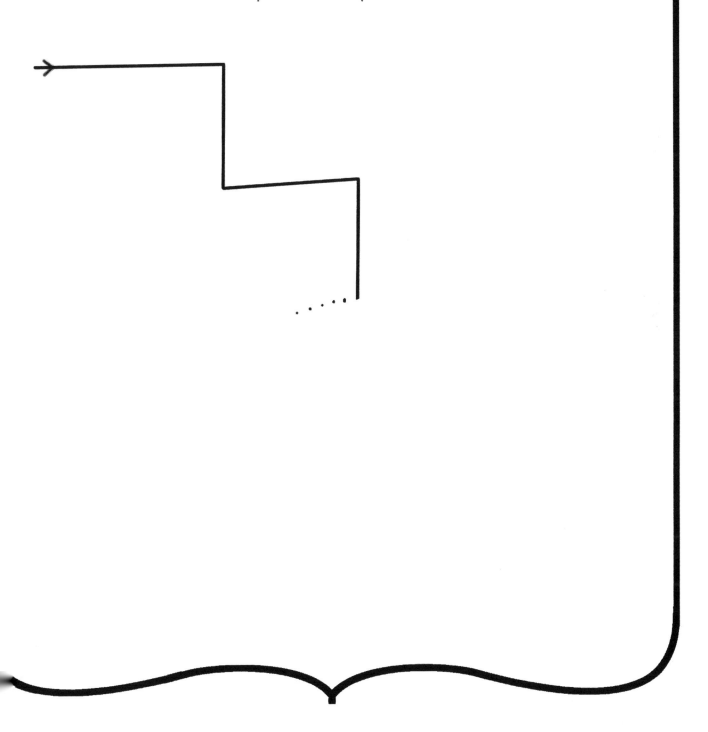

Tic - Tac - Toe

Two players decide if they want to be X or 0.
Players take turns marking the spaces in the grid with their X or 0.
The winner is the one who places three of their X's or 0's in a
horizontal, vertical, or diagonal row.

Play a Tic-Tac-Toe game in each heart grid.

Count How Many

Count how many there are;
Draw a (circle) around the number of how many you counted
Color the pictures.

1 one   2 two   3 three   4 four   5 five

6 six   7 seven   8 eight   9 nine   10 ten

Practice writing the number on the lines below.

Trace and Color Shapes

Carefully trace each shape with a crayon. or marker.
Choose another crayon and color the inside of the shape.

Square

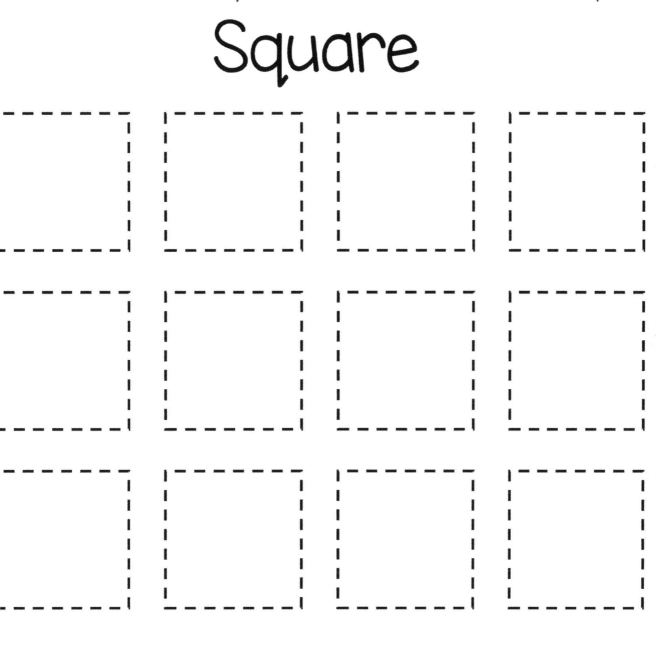

Through the Maze

Help find the way through the maze.

START

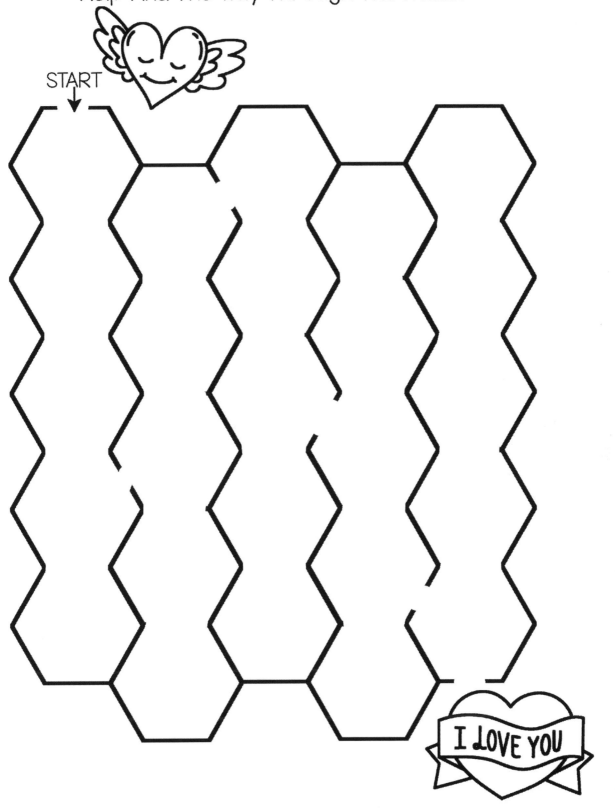

I LOVE YOU

Match The Same

Draw a line to match the pictures that are the <u>same</u>.
Color the pictures.

Drawing Curvy Lines

Trace over the line with your pencil, then keep going.
Fill the page with curvy lines.

Color the shpes that you have made.

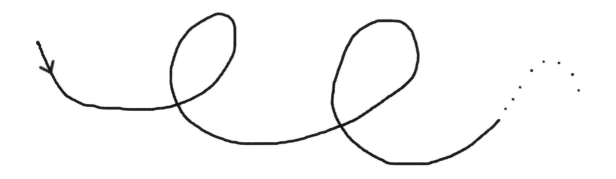

Tic - Tac - Toe

Two players decide if they want to be X or 0.
Players take turns marking the spaces in the grid with their X or 0.
The winner is the one who places three of their X's or 0's in a
horizontal, vertical, or diagonal row.

Play a Tic-Tac-Toe game in each heart grid.

Count How Many

Count how many there are;
Draw a (circle) around the number of how many you counted
Color the pictures.

1 one   2 two   3 three   4 four   5 five

6 six   7 seven   8 eight   9 nine   10 ten

Practice writing the number on the lines below.

Trace and Color Shapes

Carefully trace each shape with a crayon. or marker.
Choose another crayon and color the inside of the shape.

Circle

Through the Maze

Help find the way through the maze.

START

FINISH

Odd One Out

Look at the first picture on each line.
Draw an X on the picture that is different.
Color the pictures.

Drawing Straight Lines

Trace over the line with your pencil, then keep going.
Fill the page with straight lines.

Color the shpes that you have made.

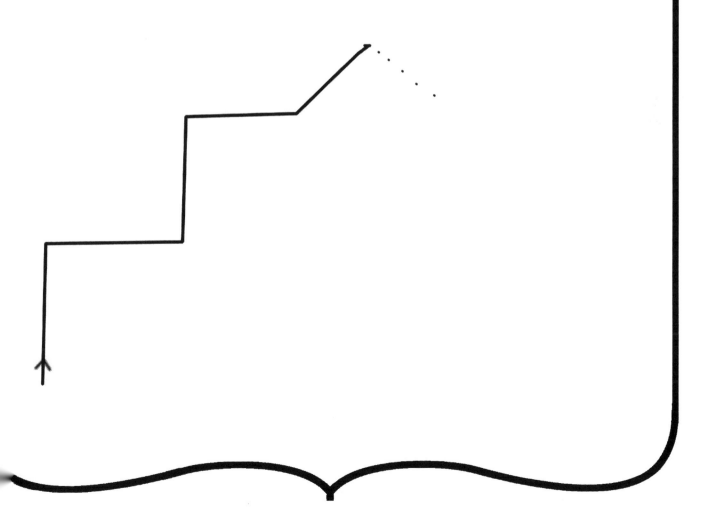

Tic - Tac - Toe

Two players decide if they want to be X or O.
Players take turns marking the spaces in the grid with their X or O.
The winner is the one who places three of their X's or O's in a
horizontal, vertical, or diagonal row.

Play a Tic-Tac-Toe game in each heart grid.

Count How Many

Count how many there are;
Draw a (circle) around the number of how many you counted
Color the pictures.

1 one   2 two   3 three   4 four   5 five

6 six   7 seven   8 eight   9 nine   10 ten

Practice writing the number on the lines below.

_____

- -

_____

Trace and Color Shapes

Carefully trace each shape with a crayon. or marker.
Choose another crayon and color the inside of the shape.

Rectangle

Through the Maze

Help find the way through the maze.

START

Match The Same

Draw a line to match the pictures that are the <u>same</u>.
Color the pictures.

Drawing Curvy Lines

Trace over the line with your pencil, then keep going.
Fill the page with curvy lines.

Color the shpes that you have made.

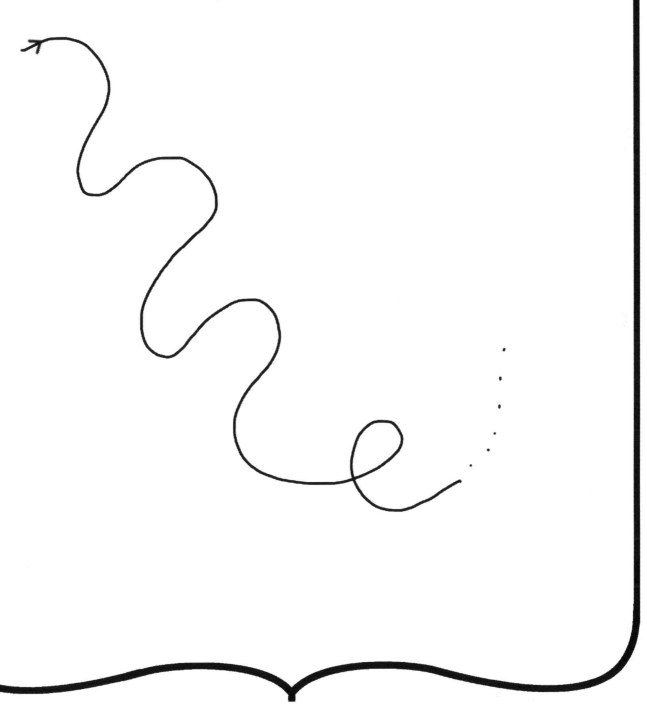

Tic - Tac - Toe

Two players decide if they want to be X or O.
Players take turns marking the spaces in the grid with their X or O.
The winner is the one who places three of their X's or O's in a
horizontal, vertical, or diagonal row.

Play a Tic-Tac-Toe game in each heart grid.

Count How Many

Count how many there are;
Draw a (circle) around the number of how many you counted
Color the pictures.

1 one 2 two 3 three 4 four 5 five

6 six 7 seven 8 eight 9 nine 10 ten

Practice writing the number on the lines below.

_____

- - - - - - - - - - - - - - - -

_____

Trace and Color Shapes

Carefully trace each shape with a crayon. or marker.
Choose another crayon and color the inside of the shape.

Oval

Through the Maze

Help find the way through the maze.

START

FINISH

Odd One Out

Look at the first picture on each line.
Draw an X on the picture that is different.
Color the pictures.

Drawing Straight Lines

Trace over the line with your pencil, then keep going.
Fill the page with straight lines.

Color the shpes that you have made.

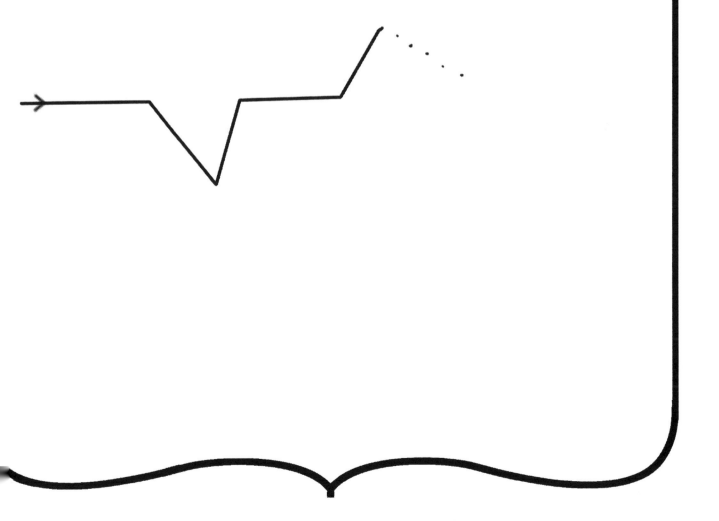

Tic - Tac - Toe

Two players decide if they want to be X or 0.
Players take turns marking the spaces in the grid with their X or 0.
The winner is the one who places three of their X's or 0's in a
horizontal, vertical, or diagonal row.

Play a Tic-Tac-Toe game in each heart grid.

Count How Many

Count how many there are;
Draw a (circle) around the number of how many you counted
Color the pictures.

1 one 2 two 3 three 4 four 5 five

6 six 7 seven 8 eight 9 nine 10 ten

Practice writing the number on the lines below.

Trace and Color Shapes

Carefully trace each shape with a crayon. or marker.
Choose another crayon and color the inside of the shape.

Hexagon

Through the Maze

Help find the way through the maze.

START

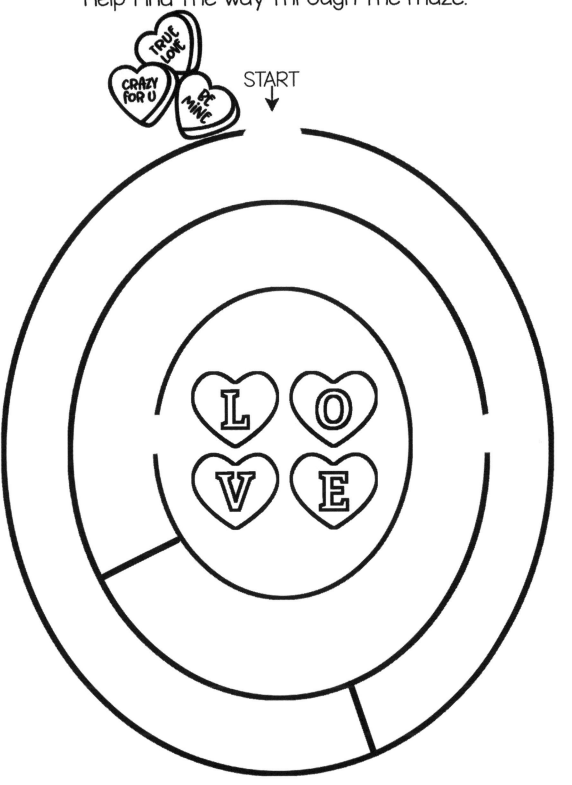

Match The Same

Draw a line to match the pictures that are the <u>same</u>.
 Color the pictures.

Drawing Curvy Lines

Trace over the line with your pencil, then keep going.
Fill the page with curvy lines.

Color the shpes that you have made.

Tic - Tac - Toe

Two players decide if they want to be X or O.
Players take turns marking the spaces in the grid with their X or O.
The winner is the one who places three of their X's or O's in a
horizontal, vertical, or diagonal row.

Play a Tic-Tac-Toe game in each heart grid.

Count How Many

Count how many there are;
Draw a (circle) around the number of how many you counted
Color the pictures.

1 one 2 two 3 three 4 four 5 five

6 six 7 seven 8 eight 9 nine 10 ten

Practice writing the number on the lines below.

_____

- - - - - - - - - - - - - - - - - - -

_____

Trace and Color Shapes

Carefully trace each shape with a crayon. or marker.
Choose another crayon and color the inside of the shape.

Trapezoid

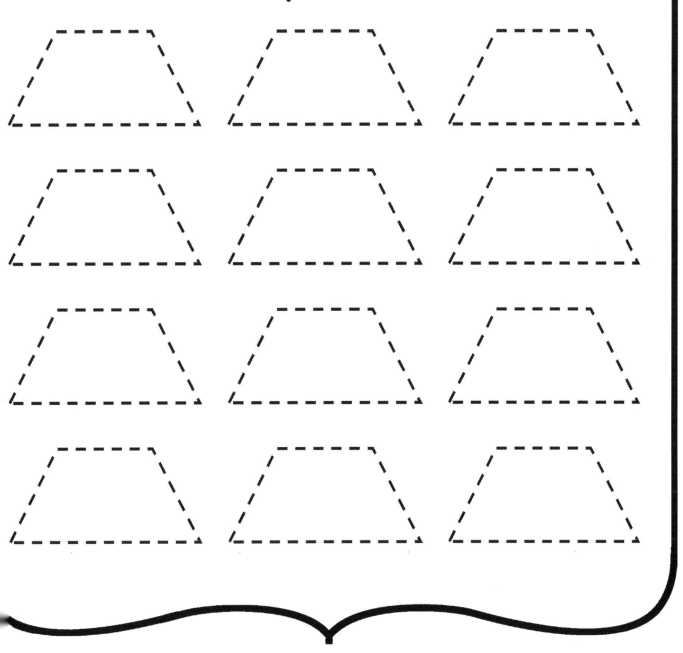

Through the Maze

Help find the way through the maze.

START

Odd One Out

Look at the first picture on each line.
Draw an X on the picture that is different.
Color the pictures.

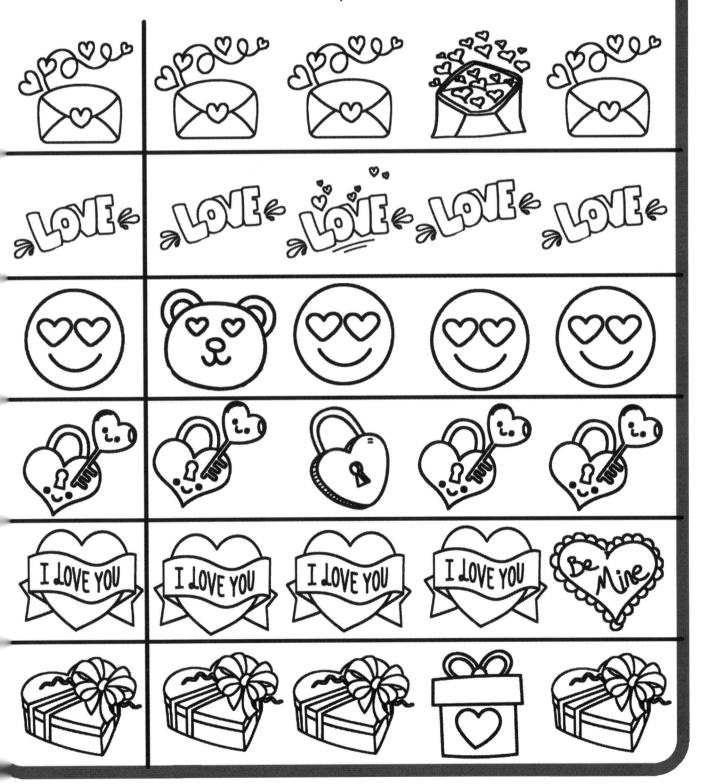

Drawing Straight Lines

Trace over the line with your pencil, then keep going.
Fill the page with straight lines.

Color the shpes that you have made.

Tic - Tac - Toe

Two players decide if they want to be X or 0.
Players take turns marking the spaces in the grid with their X or 0.
The winner is the one who places three of their X's or 0's in a
horizontal, vertical, or diagonal row.

Play a Tic-Tac-Toe game in each heart grid.

Count How Many

Count how many there are;
Draw a (circle) around the number of how many you counted
Color the pictures.

Practice writing the number on the lines below.

_____

- - - - - - - - - - - - - - - - - -

_____

Trace and Color Shapes

Carefully trace each shape with a crayon. or marker.
Choose another crayon and color the inside of the shape.

Star

Through the Maze

Help find the way through the maze.

START

FINISH

Match The Same

Draw a line to match the pictures that are the <u>same</u>.
Color the pictures.

Drawing Curvy Lines

Trace over the line with your pencil, then keep going.
Fill the page with curvy lines.

Color the shpes that you have made.

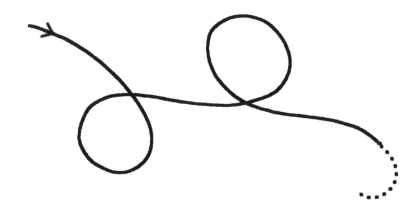

Tic - Tac - Toe

Two players decide if they want to be X or O.
layers take turns marking the spaces in the grid with their X or O.
The winner is the one who places three of their X's or O's in a
horizontal, vertical, or diagonal row.

Play a Tic-Tac-Toe game in each heart grid.

Count How Many

Count how many there are;
Draw a (circle) around the number of how many you counted
Color the pictures.

1 one   2 two   3 three   4 four   5 five

6 six   7 seven   8 eight   9 nine   10 ten

Practice writing the number on the lines below.

Trace and Color Shapes

Carefully trace each shape with a crayon. or marker.
Choose another crayon and color the inside of the shape.

Heart

Through the Maze

Help find the way through the maze.

START

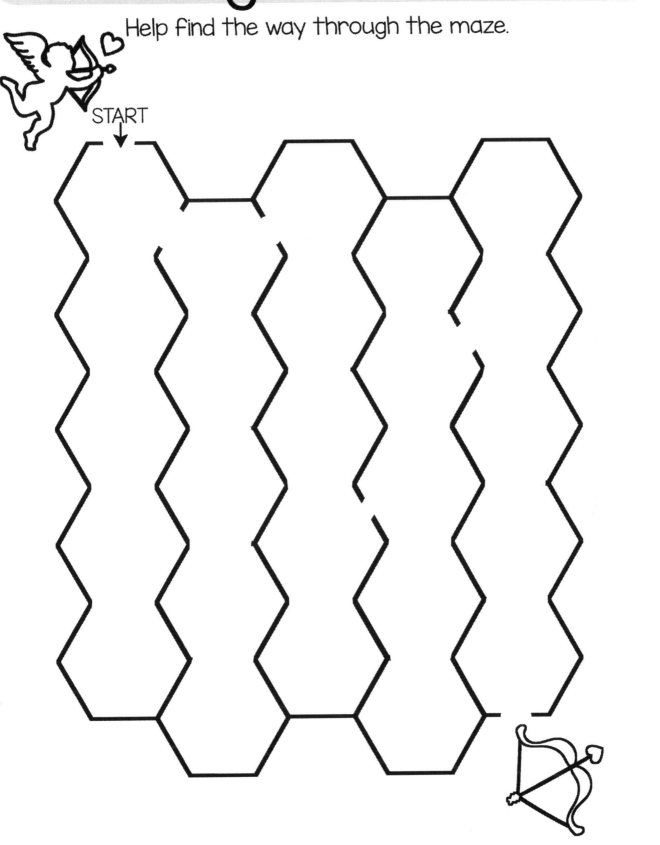

Odd One Out

Look at the first picture on each line.
Draw an X on the picture that is <u>different</u>.
Color the pictures.

Drawing Straight Lines

Trace over the line with your pencil, then keep going.
Fill the page with straight lines.

Color the shpes that you have made.

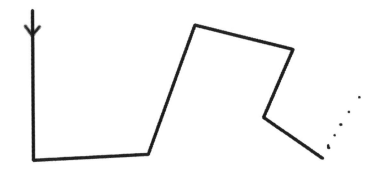

Tic - Tac - Toe

Two players decide if they want to be X or O.
Players take turns marking the spaces in the grid with their X or O.
The winner is the one who places three of their X's or O's in a
horizontal, vertical, or diagonal row.

Play a Tic-Tac-Toe game in each heart grid.

Made in the USA
Middletown, DE
29 December 2020

30406218R00091